THE PORTAGE POETRY
SERIES

Series Titles

The Green Vault Heist
David Salner

There is a Corner of Someplace Else
Camden Michael Jones

Everything Waits
Jonathan Graham

We Are Reckless
Christy Prahl

Always a Body
Molly Fuller

Bowed As If Laden With Snow
Megan Wildhood

Silent Letter
Gail Hanlon

New Wilderness
Jenifer DeBellis

Fulgurite
Catherine Kyle

The Body Is Burden and Delight
Sharon White

Bone Country
Linda Nemec Foster

Not Just the Fire
R.B. Simon

Monarch
Heather Bourbeau

The Walk to Cefalù
Lynne Viti

Praise for

Listening to Mars

"In *Listening to Mars*, we find Sally Ashton at the height of her poetic powers, juxtaposing prose and verse poems and melding intellectual and scientific history with autobiography to explore the struggles we face when confronted daily by the miraculous and terrifying universe we inhabit. The uncertainties and frightening images of Covid's early rampage also hover over this book, with the poet eventually emerging from her cocoon in the final poem—a poem that suggests a Sisyphean acceptance of our precarious place in the cosmos. 'To pick up again,' she writes, 'and head out an open door. It is to reawaken, to leave behind the dream life, trade it for, yes, life to live, to lose.'"

—Peter Johnson
author of *While the Undertaker Sleeps: Collected and New Prose Poems*

"Listening is the quietest of talents, and the most fruitful. In this moving collection, Sally Ashton brings to readers what she heard as time and space had their way with us during the early years of the pandemic. In these poems, she creates Einsteinian thought experiments, tools for understanding and enduring the grief and beauty of a world where 'nothing stands still.' Loss and wonder, dread and awe gyrate throughout the book, spinning like heavenly bodies, the poet equally rigorous and tender in her search for 'words that make the world look like what it feels like.' Ashton reveres the mysterious movement of the world and offers it as a comfort: 'While Earth kept turning, gravity held us close.'"

—Holly Iglesias
author of *Angles of Approach*

"Sally Ashton's *Listening to Mars* beguiles and wonders. Its poignant, glistering poems meditate on beauty and sadness in equal measure, considering the ineffable and absorbing glories of the cosmos, the Covid pandemic and its aftermath, and the importance of a fully engaged quotidian life. These are subtly crafted, salutary and lyrical examinations of belonging, alienation and the power of memory. They are tough and excruciatingly delicate, with an attentive tenderness—'clear, hot, with a chance of sorrow.' Ashton is recognised internationally for her use of the free line and in *Listening to Mars*, she uses this mode in thrilling ways to explore philosophies of the neo-sublime. I urge you to follow Ashton's brilliant, transportive works through their powerful considerations of time's exigencies and their valuing of human care and proximity."

—Cassandra Atherton
co-author of *Prose Poetry: An Introduction*

"What does it mean to be human in the late Anthropocene, when we can send 'rockets to Mars' but must sing operas to potted plants, when zucchini grows 'mad in the garden' but our children fear killing us by coming home for dinner? Ashton's bighearted new collection explores this fertile ground through poems that transport us nimbly from backyard lawn chair to the 'alien wind/singing its deep melody into space.' These are poems of witty watchfulness, mystery at the brink of ruin, and sustained delight in the 'kabillioness/of it all' that you simply won't want to miss."

—Annie Kim
author of *Eros Unbroken*

LISTENING
TO **MARS**

POEMS

SALLY
ASHTON

CORNERSTONE PRESS
UNIVERSITY OF WISCONSIN-STEVENS POINT

Cornerstone Press, Stevens Point, Wisconsin 54481
Copyright © 2024 Sally Ashton
www.uwsp.edu/cornerstone

Printed in the United States of America by
Point Print and Design Studio, Stevens Point, Wisconsin

Library of Congress Control Number: 2023951986
ISBN: 978-1-960329-26-4

Cover photograph © NASA

Cornerstone Press titles are produced in courses and internships offered by the
Department of English at the University of Wisconsin–Stevens Point.

DIRECTOR & PUBLISHER
Dr. Ross K. Tangedal

EXECUTIVE EDITORS
Jeff Snowbarger, Freesia McKee

EDITORIAL DIRECTOR
Ellie Atkinson

SENIOR EDITORS
Brett Hill, Grace Dahl

PRESS STAFF
Carolyn Czerwinski, Sophie McPherson, Eva Nielsen, Natalie Reiter, Ava Willett

for Frank,
who was there all along, listening

CONTENTS

We ourselves are both actors and spectators
in the drama of existence.

—Niels Bohr

There are more individual viruses on planet earth than stars in the
Universe.

—Science Friday

Let me see what spring is like
On Jupiter and Mars

—Frank Bart

Fiction, 101

Start at the moment when everything changes.

If nothing changes, what's the story?

The main character will be a most unlikely person.

Desire drives the action.

Show, don't tell, Chekhov admonished, *don't tell me the moon is shining, show me the glint of light on broken glass.*

It's a hero's journey, the way full of unseen dangers, your hero unprepared.

If she comes to a river, it will be muddy, wide, full of crocodiles.

Make sure to show the glint of light on broken water, the crocodile's eyes unblinking.

The story won't end, *She wakes up. It was only a dream.*

If she drowns or crocodiles tear her apart, the story becomes tragedy.

If she sits down refusing to go on, it's tragedy of another sort.

And she *will* wake up—many times—sometimes after dreaming, but the crocodiles are always there.

Her only escape is to cross the river. She has no idea how.

The story will get worse before it gets better.

In the nick of time, help arrives.

When this is all over, the world too will be changed.

Don't tell me the moon is shining . . .

I will see the broken glass.

Show me, if you can, the glint of light.

California, April

Turkey spreads his feathers.
I rearrange the sorrow

For Valentine's Day,

which I don't believe in, you took me to the coast and I took you there too because we are lovers, but we are egalitarian. To the coast we went, a "dreamy divagation" Elizabeth Bishop once wrote of her day's-end bus ride, but you drove the Subaru divagating through mountains until our journey turned from west to north to wander up Highway 1 along the coast past artichoke fields, strawberry stands, the herds of lucky cows half the size of a moose, lucky cows to dream and graze sea-salted fields at land's end until their luck runs out, as it will for each of us, in that car or reading this page. O, Valentine a dream-like distant hour we slurped Duarte's famed green-chili soup, and I stole one handful of polished stones from the forbidden beach we visited afterward that year before everything became forbidden, the drive, the beach, the restaurant we lingered in, bowls of public soup, life as we'd always lived it—common as the cows' grassy daze—lost what we'd known and counted on, our three beloved friends and oh my heart, the millions more still to be lost since Valentine's Day.

To Calculate the Color of the Sky

*. . . a lot of ancient languages did not have a specific word for blue.
Not having a word for the color blue suggests that our ancestors did
not see blue at all.*

—Lucy Huang

Maybe I'm approaching apogee.

My mother missing eternally; my brother gone for less than a year.

March. Stay-at-home orders to "flatten the curve."

I start a pandemic blog. I last two weeks.

My husband plays loud music, fries bacon. "This is fun," he says,
sitting down with me for lunch.

At CVS the unmasked checker, whistling, licks her fingertips to
grab my bag.

My husband suggests a walk.

Is our DNA changing?

My friend Nellie's cancer numbers skyrocket.

The loud whir of silence.

Flatten the curve comes to mean the rate of panic.

April

Excelsior. E pluribus unum.

I long for presence, for the many who I now must not see.

Though I *could.*

Judith, dying in Seattle, sends a farewell letter.

The shadow of nothing is a black hole.

On Facebook I discover a friend from work has died.

Whales in the shipping lanes, wild goats on city streets. A mountain lion yawns in a backyard tree.

The daughters send pictures of Judith's green burial.

What day is it?

We drive to the beach, reopened, the sun on the waves as if nothing has happened.

Absence can't be imagined until it comes.

It could be an ordinary warm spring day.

May. Poppies nod in the backyard.

A morning text, Nellie died overnight.

The house full of shadows, outside it's a hologram.

I have talked to myself my whole life. I also talk to the dead.

All the same and everything different.

Minneapolis, WTF? Everyone a bystander, none of us innocent.

June. My daughter at last proposes a bubble.

I write a fable about a woman and her magic hat.

When my husband cuts his own hair, I think *he* needs a magic hat.

In the yard, peaches ripen.

The sky remains huge and reliably wonderful, someone says.

At least it's wonderfully reliable, I think.

This Is What It Looked Like When We Got There

so we did the best we could. A string quartet performed to an audience of potted plants that filled the seats through all five balconies of the opera house. At the end of Puccini the plants applauded, waving and rasping their leaves together. In churches priests taped hand-drawn faces of absent parishioners along vacant pews to keep themselves company. Human avatars tuned in from home, lined up on screens. A plastic rain fell. Elsewhere, we knew about the refrigerated trucks. Elsewhere it was summer, the world in full-leaf. Zucchini grew mad in the garden, more than anyone wanted to eat. Not wanting to kill us, our children refused to come inside, then they wouldn't visit at all. No, we didn't want our grandchildren to live with such knowledge either, but we were running out of time. Whenever we checked, it was two o'clock Thursday. The symbolic stage. A woman working at a call center in India mentioned she had three roosters in her yard. The discord was earsplitting. We looked for *Neowise*, sent rockets to Mars. We were on our way to a new world we could barely imagine, a long-short autumn lay ahead, and we weren't going anywhere else.

Quarantine

Tu, che di gel sei cinta

And it was like that opera singer confined aboard her virus-infected cruise ship circling the Golden Gate just in sight of land subsisting on leftover cold eggs and stale French toast, waiting all day for a crew member to deliver a ration of toilet paper. Trapped aboard that floating Alcatraz welcome nowhere, her shipmates argued politics while hidden behind their balconies' partitions. She stood on her balcony and sang over their cursing. She sang to the sea, to the heavens, to herself, an aria from Puccini's "Turandot." It was the part where the slave girl pleads with the merciless queen to soften her heart, *Listen to me You, who are girdled with ice*, but alas, realizing there would be no mercy, the slave girl pulls out a knife and kills herself right there. "I just want to get off the boat," the singer told a reporter. "Can't you get me off this boat?"

This Was Also True

People began to die. We were forbidden to see. *Wash frequently*, authorities said. House arrest followed. I was separated from my children. We were warned not to drive except to find food. Grocery shelves emptied. *There will be no shortages*, they insisted though I couldn't find soap, beans, rice. We were required to wear masks and cry out "Unclean! Unclean!" if anyone approached. *Touch no one*, they said. If touched, I removed my clothing, washed repeatedly, left my shoes outside. We were forbidden to cut our hair, take food among strangers. Our husbands no longer shaved. Women went gray before our eyes. Screens monitored everyone. People died anyway. The president said, "It's almost over." The doctors said, "It has only begun."

After many weeks, we were forced to watch the execution of an innocent man in slow motion, over and over. The images ran night and day. The executioner took a knee, looked me in the eye, hand tucked in his left pocket. The dying man whispered "Please." I watched his urine trail across the sidewalk. "Don't speak," his executioner instructed. As I've said, I saw this many times. Enough is never enough. But now it was too much. People escaped from their houses. Millions filled the streets. The president washed his hands. "This must stop," he said. "But it has only begun," the people replied.

Litany in a Time of Contagion

You should know a river, the science of it, its stones, its coursing repetitions. Its silences. Its constant presence, *come in, come in.* To be curious, to notice. To learn this relationship. To jump from one rock to another while your legs can still carry you there. Before once upon a time. (Lord, have mercy on us) To watch an ancient fisherman tie a fly twisting horsehair with feather from a mockingbird's breast, the movement of line and current, a copper-speckled body held, returned. (Christ, have mercy on us) To interpret feathers and what is born in the stream. To know the world changes in an instant. (Lord, have mercy on us) Gather everything, the lived things, the lost place. Find it—stay alive. (Amen)

The Still Center of the Galaxy

I'm listening to the fountain plash, watching the hornbeams tussle with the breeze, feeling time melt into birdsong, and then the drone of a plane crossing overhead. I'm staring at middle distance and a shadow moving on the wall. The sun moves imperceptibly though then I remember it really doesn't move at all. Life is the dream I'm having in the middle of the day. It won't always be like this, all the furniture motionless. Things don't move unless I move them. My linen shirt hangs straight down from a single dresser knob. Nothing stands still.

Looking for a Resurrection

You start where you can—
next to a yellow ladder
under a bee-filled arbor.

You feel you might
              fly away
on their strong engines' roar.

A new green hose ropes
around itself in hopeful coils.
Pruning shears, garden fork, rake

hang on nails driven into the fence.
You take the shovel, open
earth's damp side, place

dark seed in the wound
made there to prove
you're still alive.

A jigger of June,

Siri transposes, maybe wanting to mix things another way, tired of the usual, tired of all of us these dog and cat days unmarked by the miraculous who seek solace in spirits, different kinds different times, hoping for antibodies against fire, flood, drought, hurricane, plague, so that when someone mentions a swarm of locusts is expected tomorrow I wonder how I could possibly have missed it in my newsfeed, no longer attuned to irony, what's it good for anyway now that nothing seems to come as a surprise, but here's to a jigger of June like a tune we all mostly remember though we've lost the words—something, something, moon?—I hum instead, fill the glass with ice, squeeze lime over, dump in gin, tonic, no longer bothering to measure.

Transit

My house floats free under June's full Moon, abandoned for the forest primeval. To live in a tent, build fires, listen to a river roar, I wanted things that make sense when someone dies. Left alone, the house also wept. Tears streamed from light switches, buckled the floorboards, seeped into the sheetrock the way grief cannot be mopped up nor contained. The way it remains soggy underfoot. The way it wouldn't flee from me, chased by flashlights, stars, and the dark shapes of bears. So I pack up the car, come home to my house, find it unmoored. I climb aboard anyway, captain of my catastrophes, of curled carpet and mildewed luggage, all hands on deck, grief a yellow-legged parrot perched on my shoulder calling for crackers, digging its claws in at every lurch, the roar of many waters—man overboard—everything rocking, even the Moon going under. I lean against a window frame, the universe—so vast! This sea so unforgivably wide.

July, How Far I Fly

Yes, there were hundreds of satellites to keep track of. Yes, a jet rumbled on its course from time to time, but clocks on Earth had begun to follow a curious logic, so who knew. They called it a Metal Rat Year. I never found out what that meant, but it sounded right. Somewhere deep in the house footsteps could be heard crossing, recrossing the hardwood. Somewhere a dog barked. It seemed endless. I turned the page, nothing lasts forever. Something about the law of nature, something about the dream of man. A fine-tuned car alarm blasted one note for several uninterrupted minutes, then silence. Nothing lasts. Turn the page. Turn the page, which was how I sometimes read the world. Pretty much everything in space spins, and now I felt it at the quantum level. How long could I hold my breath? July clear, hot, with a chance of sorrow, but honey, that was just life in the late Anthropocene.

Terra Incognita, September

I am a model citizen.

Circumferences

When home was a closed circle inside an iron gate.

When I spoke to lizards, advising them, looking for advice.

When I was seen to consort with crows.

A day should be more than a list.

Proof of disappearing: an airport drop-off, a single dinner plate.

Rocketship goodbyes.

When I watched for rabbits, coaxed the quail to stay with handfuls of tossed seed.

When I memorized the slippage of stars.

When a coyote's hunting song tore at the nights.

There were one hundred ways of looking out a window.

The heart complained, forever elsewhere.

We spoke by pixel and digit.

I made a steady stream of alterations.

We sent each other hours of photos.

When leaves told stories I couldn't comprehend.

When I could not cajole the rain nor coerce the snow to fall.

When I knew the landscape of my childhood had forever changed.

Owls too came near at night.

By day, the titmouse built a nest in the birdhouse, the crow in the cypress, the rabbit in the rosemary, but the owlhouse yawned, its door a vacant "o."

As with any apocalypse, lizards, birds, and spiders thrived.

How I reckoned by the Moon, its constantly inconstant circle.

Moon of Little Long Day Night.

A circle like the "o" in hope traced over and over.

The circle was the "o" in hollow, in echo, in home, perfectly empty.

A Question While Watching Birds

Who came to the birdfeeder just now,
  who came tail-tapping

startling with a buzzing cry the wide-eyed dove prodding the
ground beneath? Who came in the still-hot evening, two days
before the longest day of this unexpected year. Oh, this motionless
light. Did I say still? The evening at a standstill holding all breath
waiting for some change. The birds, tiny dinosaurs, what can they
tell of change, of making it through? A hummingbird helicopters
out of sight.

*

Goldfinch, Lesser Goldfinch,
  Chestnut-backed Chickadee.

Wilson's Warbler, swallows spin against the eaves. On occasion in
late spring, a treetop fledged with Cedar Waxwings.

*

In May, robins sing
their hearts out, then disappear
cliché, cliché, cliché.

*

It's a bird . . . it's a spacecraft . . .
  it's "Hope" sent to Mars,
somehow appropriate.

*

Emily Dickinson once wrote
Hope is the thing with feathers.

Watching all these months, I hope to understand.

*

I discover a dead dove
        on the step below the kitchen window
red feet curled into her breast.

When I step closer, her mate startles out of a nearby bush. She's
still limp when I lift her into a plastic bag, carry her to the trash.

*

Distant mockingbird
        rehearses 7:30 a.m.

It's come down to copying aphorisms from newspaper articles.
Gavin Cosgrave advocates we "meander from grief to gratitude." I
spend too much time looking down. I meander toward the dinner
dishes soaking since last night.

*

I miss the world.

*

The Moon is flying—
        no, that's just a seagull

*I wish I could come up and grab you. I would put you where I can
always find you,* my small grandson sings in a video, pointing to a
corner of his backyard, so far from mine. The Moon's silvered
arms hold everything lost, I tell the video. The seagull wheels
away

*

Titmouse with a mohawk,
    Bewick's Wren . . .

*

And *if a thrush on a branch*
    is not a sign,

as Miłosz reckoned, *But just a thrush on the branch,* or just a
goldfinch at our feeder, or a dove patient below, or just an army of
hummingbirds filling time with a fury of wings and darting cries,
am I simply a one-time prisoner stranded behind a kitchen window
noting what I can, marking what remains?

*

tweyee, eh-eh-eng,
    ji-ji-ji
sweetie-sweetie-sweetie

*

Google any bird's song
    and you'll find a recording.

My husband discovers he can lure the birds. I see the way he leans
far into the empty evenings holding up his phone, face open to the
sky, replaying a shrill call, both of us expectant, waiting for any
reply.

Insomnia Remix

Haiku moon tonight—
I lie awake until dawn
counting syllables

Haiku moon tonight—
I lie awake until dawn.
Awake tonight, moon haiku,
I lie until dawn
counting syllables.

Counting syllables
the crickets chant in the dark.
Crickets counting, chanting
syllables in the dark—
a night full of stars.

A night full of stars.
No sleep. Each hour numbered.
A no-sleep night full of hours
each numbered star—
stars like polished flames.

Stars like polished flames—
Earth turns past them in the dark.
Earth turns. Past it, stars like flames
polishing the dark
proximate and strange.

Proximate and strange
what I see from my window.
Strange, proximate window and
what I see from it—
Moon above treetops.

Moon above treetops
imaginary river.
Treetops, Moon's river above—
imagining it
my pen makes night work.

My pen makes night work
everyone else sound asleep.
Work. The pen makes its night sound—
everyone else sleeps
tonight, haiku moon.

Last Flight Out

It would have to be
perfect timing it's
completely unheard of
wouldn't it be a magical
occurrence smaller odds
than a lucky lottery ticket
a little spooky it is
impossible to imagine it
would be difficult to photograph
while flying a helicopter
while fighting a fire while
dumping water on flames
on the forest below it would
need to be flying at just the right
speed it requires the same speed
to fly under those blades
a miracle of navigation to make
it inside to land on the seat
back right next to the pilot
who said he was startled
who said *please* to the owl
please don't attack me
the owl staring at him perched
silent beside him such a chill
co-pilot must have given
the pilot some seconds of
breath-stopping wonder
flown out of a furnace
of flames the sky blinded
by smoke filled with deafening
engines of wind-whipping
copters the owl sat observing
a couple more water dumps
dropped over the treetops
then left the way it came

according to the pilot
who *had* snapped a photo
from inside the cockpit
later showed a reporter
which of course made
the news we were California
on fire incinerating for weeks
particulate deaths in the air—
I bought an air purifier.
Later I saw the owl's photo
online steady eyes yellow
caught there in the lens
lucky moment before it flew
back out into it what did it
know did it know there would be
no real escape for any of us?

October 31,

as the crow flies, over the group of street folk gathered under a potted tree near a garbage can across the square.

As the crow flies over the yellowed mulberry leaves-like-hands fallen at last from late trees.

As the crow flies across the end of the day.

Looking noble, looking like a spy.

As the crow flies, past the kitten and the ninja warrior.

As the crow flies over the father and his children, past the woman who carries her bedroll, over the city's sunless canyon and the boys—thirteen autumns old—wearing masks.

Over heads, over treetops, out from the city.

Flying past us into sunset, flying feathers that keep it aloft in spite of lightness and silence.

What does it see?

Beating toward midnight as the crow flies.

Something clutched in yellow feet, a last crust of daylight dropping from its beak.

Quantum Sense

A flash, rust-gray. Call it deep mind. Ears and probes, bird as spacecraft, seeing with feathers. Feel astonishment. To read light. To follow the magnetic field, Earth's poles entangled in their cells signaling a flightpath, the way of return no matter how far away they are, beckoned, something like lights on a runway. As faithful as the steps of cattle. Electrons spin correspondingly, a compass of light inside the robin's eye, a bright place you will never see into or out of, a ring of white feathers. You wish you could re-member. A certainty. A way of being. The robin cocks its head, a vanished moment, silent out of sight, empty branch, wings into another sky.

for JP

Winter Rhetoric #21

The long winter begins
a spray of mandarin oranges
a pair of juncos happy
below the birdfeeder mock me
the winter thirteen days old
snow falling in Berlin I am
in California a seven second
video you can hear the flakes
hiss a spray of mandarins resting
on the table mocking juncos
foreboding strangers in line
waiting for deliverance
each day like returning from
Mars will I be older younger
changed at the cellular level
orange mandarins wet green
leaves I have read most of the
Sunday *New York Times* I pull
the lights from the brave
Christmas tree's limbs it's only
10 o'clock winter just beginning

"The polar vortex is about to split again . . ."

. . . otherwise it will be
a typical Covid lock-
down January bright
with a threat of violence
an average chance of
revolution a hint of mutiny
increasing overnight
will bring highs of panic
in spite of locking the
barn after the horse
is gone we are anticipating
an unseasonal threat amid
whispers of a conspiracy
cloudy with possible arrests
following ominous silence
look for a failure of
intelligence in spite
of a gathering storm more
fog in the forecast
caused by high pressure
building with no break
in the protests a clear
and present danger predicted
over much of the nation
another more robust split
our meteorologist reports
will set the stage we
want no violence, no violence
never any violence the
president said elsewhere

Looking at Mars with Stevens

I
After fourteen weeks of lockdown
The news that caught my eye
Was three space missions to Mars.

II
I was of three minds,
Like the sky
In which three rockets race to Mars.

III
Mars in transit across the night sky.
It was my insomnia obsession.

IV
The sky and a woman
Are one.
The sky and a woman and planet Mars
Are one.

V
I don't know what's more alarming,
Jeff Bezos' space conquest
Or Elon Musk's Martian colonies,
Mars as an outpost
Or a backup.

VI
Constellations crossed the window,
Relentless clockwork.
Mars-the-red, lonely cipher,
Followed them every night.
The Moon
Winced through its phases
Already conquered, a lost cause.

VII
O rich men, O humans,
Why imagine replacement planets?
Have you seen the surface of Mars,
A Waste Land, no air?
You can't even walk outside.

VIII
I know the noble names,
Perseverance, Hope, Questions to Heaven.
But I know, too,
That planet Mars is not
In what I know.

IX
When the spacecrafts landed on Mars
It was the dead
Of the next lockdown winter.

X
If they had to live there
Beneath the reddened sun
The pimps of disinformation
Might sing a new song.

XI
She rode out the Pandemic
In a time warp.
Often it seemed like
A science fiction,
Like "Groundhog's Day," but waking up
On Mars.

XII
Now we're moving backwards.
Mars must be in retrograde.

XIII
It was Thursday every day.
It never rained.
And I wanted it to rain.
Mars kept circling,
A distant red light.

Sky Writing

What remains to be written of this year will need a cloudless sky and the acrobatic courage of a stunt pilot twisting through runes to wrestle language from smoke. It will need a still afternoon, one from September, with that kind of blue that snaps to attention. Make it something a child can read, good news instead of threats—*surrender Dorothy*—that darkened other skies. No tornado, no wind. Use words that make amends.

Horizonless

When I open the door, the bee flies in again.
Elsewhere, the Universe is expanding.

Listening to Mars,

ear pressed to my laptop's
small speaker that replays a recording
captured by seismometer, a bass tone
drones some 140 million miles from Earth,
kabillion being another useful term
because "Martian wind" seems a kabillion
million miles from anything I know, gusting
unseen across the parched red surface only
accidentally captured by the InSight lander's
equipment instead tuned to intercept signals
from Mars's deep interior, a seismic pulse
that will say something about the planet's
inner space, the kind of low frequency waves
whales and elephants can hear, though
elephants hear through their feet,
sound traveling through their giant
toenails to the ear via bone
while whales' tiny ears sift the deep
for sound vibrations the way their massive
mouths sift volumes of water for also-invisible
krill, at the same time we're messing them
up with underwater sonar blasts like
we've messed up our own atmosphere
with radio waves so that the only peaceful
place free of frequency noise
where we might hear from the Universe
is on the far side of the Moon—
once called "dark" because we'd never seen it—
where China just landed a mooncraft to listen
to what might come from that great stillness,
such as the repeating fast radio blasts
from some distant galaxy detected by Canadian
astronomers who describe the bursts as the
"wah wah wah wah" of a sad trombone,
and it is this immensity, the kabillioness

of it all that keeps me sitting here
on the dark side of everything, motionless
next to my laptop, a type of spacecraft,
hitting replay, straining to hear an alien wind
singing its deep melody through space.

Lunacy

On clear nights
when I go outside
and the Moon is up
I call to it "Moonie!"
in a high-pitched voice
the one I use for babies
and the cat, calling as if
the Moon swelled so fine
had appeared just to greet
me at such times I'm not
so lonely thinking about
the dead who no longer
light up to see me who
won't hear me call out
their names into the
silences of space
like a fool

4.6 Billion Years

Scrolling down, reading news of the galaxy. The sun will last at most another five billion years when it will run out of fuel, become a red giant incinerating its own planetary system—us. Earth, our moon, our known fellow-planets and their myriad moons, whatever else wanders in interstellar space, vaporized—who cares about the exact science—it's the fact there's a predictable *kapow* versus an imagined eternal existence. This puts our solar system's lifespan roughly at its midpoint, a point my own life can no longer be said to occupy. Middle-aged galaxy. I'm at the 2/3 point at least. Another 30 not-improbable years to go before my own for-sure demise. In planetary years, I'm older than the sun, a good second half of its life still ahead, and Earth's with it, barring incoming asteroid or global self-annihilation. My god, I am older than the sun.

Somewhere, Midnight

I couldn't stay up to watch the night sky dazzle. I couldn't keep watch, not even for an hour. How can anyone go on seeing and seeing what's impossible in the end not to forget, like anything glimpsed from a train's window: river gorge, abandoned lot, even those kids who waved from a yard in a small Indiana town. A second later—gone, like the sky that one night over somewhere in Utah—a kaleidoscope of stars twisting. Uncountable. I pulled the curtain and slept.

Quantum Migration

It's a peculiar morning of signs, one of many. Mars' ancient riverbed appears, riven trail of pebbles and sand, and still the Moon's synchronous rotation hides its far side from us. We will never see from Earth. So it seems we must go to both these places, planet, satellite, the speculation that is space travel. To see for ourselves. To touch with our cameras, to feel with metal avatars, to listen for the sounds of stars rushing through the skies like the sound the air makes rushing past bare ears. Maybe we're seeking a geography for loss, the geometry and calculus, our missing equation? Maybe we don't know what it is we need to know, only the gravitational pull, the magnetic spin of the unknown reverberating there, repeating in the hollow center of our bones.

Everything is Moving Away from Everything Else

What else to call the great emptiness in which we live but "god" and how inscrutable the whoosh-whoosh-whoosh of a fetal heartbeat or that an artery in your friend's head bursts and a heartbeat just as suddenly stops. You used to believe God was in the heavens as someone wrote, but it's just more galaxies that lie beyond the Milky Way a few tens of millions of light-years out there, a long way to travel in search of paradise. Even the universe accelerates away from where you still sit at the kitchen table reading about the Webb Space Telescope and deep-sky objects, trying to understand. Maybe death is like a star's collapse, a gasp in the ancient galactic sky—a life implodes, energy shocks outward, light waves pulsed from a dying star—

           redshift, blueshift,
              we draw closer
      how we're pulled apart

Arboreal

Geese passed over.
I saw the sun set,
the moon rise,
a star fall.

Now in early light
the geese return
low and loud
over the orchard,

a kind of waiting broken
by impatient jay
and curt statements
of hidden birds.

Other treetops
find light first
until the sun clears
the top of the hill

and I see how light enters,
how it floods and recedes.
To be so close
to the thing but not have

the thing itself.
The grass shining,
the cows slow
and gentle voiced.

Buddha Holds Up the Earth

You must stand gently. Earth
　presses against your foot. A
breath inhaled the hands palm-up
　lift past the belly the chest
then flip to push skyward at
　shoulder-height, still the breath
sucked in until the rising hands
　meet overhead. Hold there
as if you are the Buddha as
　if your lifted hands do hold
the world's weight unlike
　Atlas crushed forever beneath
its unending curvature, its pain.
　Flip palms down and push
your breath out a slow release
　past your head your heart
something moving with them.
　Hands cup again below, empty
full ready for the next
　inhalation to rise once more
as you rise each new day
　not Buddha or any of those
names, just you, your breath
　your hands your thoughts rising
falling hold up the Earth.

Surviving Solstice

i

What now, the end of day sighs into the leaves a last shudder. The wind is alone and the birds, strange cacophony, alone too. One more mile possible, one more task or kiss or walk around the block before time ticks its heels, the world thrusts headlong toward some morning where these dishes stack clean in the cupboard I open, take in my hands, and set around the table once again.

ii

The summer of so much dying sat in the car and wouldn't get out until it was good and ready then it rattled through the cat's teeth, made her hair stand away from her body. Her spine enumerated every sorrow. She went blind, her claws frayed. This was just the cat, not our own kind. We received the news as you'd expect. At first no one could believe it. Then we made lunch and ate everything.

iii

Thirsty Dog, the dog barks a full moon madness no one resists. Mosquitoes close in and sprinklers whine far into farther hours. All life hums, freeway, sorrow, the course of blood through my veins. Even in the grave something stirs.

iv

A return to summer nights what we hold our breath for. Watching for the Moon our due portion like an evening glass of wine you wait for all day. Moonlight splashes up the sides. A fine drunkenness, every step a stagger. Unbearable this intoxication, the desire to go no further, impossible to resist each mellowing shadow.

The Unreached Paradise of our Despair

Lord Byron

N

This train is moving, always North.

So many greens.

I want to live in a tent and eat breakfast.

The needle trembles, I follow, the way sunflowers track the sun,
the way geese pass overhead.

How often I have dreamed of flying.

Past the windows dark pines rush, open on a snowy field, close like
curtains again.

I rub a circle in the foggy glass, search the sky for Northern Lights.

What is True North?

Train tracks converge in the distance, the horizon a vanishing point
of every desire.

Silence waits, the destination of each unspoken dream.

E

To go East is to return, places
of origin just outside of Eden.

East is where rivers swarmed, fish
plucked from the waters with bare hands.

We built our first homes there, trees
so plentiful we could only construct an empire.

Abundant fish, some sort of slavery
necessary. A belief at the center.

We fashioned myths in the East. Many believed,
hurried West leaving everything behind.

It's possible to go further East, where today
is just a yesterday that no one acknowledges.

Somewhere else is always West of here
so that anyone can be East. Understand?

You reach the Far East by traveling East
or West. Oceans block either journey

therefore we wonder where we're going.
How did we get here, is there hope for return.

S

Somewhere below the equator stretches a sky she has never seen,
entire continents on which she hasn't stood, unfamiliar scent
weights the air, where the sun slips quickly from the day and
feral calls sound into sleepless night, native stars, whole islands,
jungles untamed while she studies charts, follows latitudes with
her finger. The suspiration of sails, a shift in the rigging, a sud-
den lurch seaward. Somewhere, her pulse a beating drum.

W

Pressed against the Pacific all my days
I bear an imprint of coastline
like a map of the brain. Wired, valleys
creased in my flesh, phototropic,

I search for a third coast, a horizon
that circles ever out of reach, like the dome
of my skull, like the shell of heaven.
I cast about from this center, the fixed leg

of a compass. Widening, narrowing,
I measure the distances needed
to move from homeland to heartland,
the angle of escape. So many places

to belong. The pull of gravity
rooted in this chair, or strapped
in the seat of a plane, or trotting down
concrete steps to the subway. I push

the compass outward, wide as the open sea,
drawing back in on itself, an inversion,
the configuration of my beginning
moves West, and West again.

for H.B.

"We Are Going."

#NASA, Artemis Mission

We're getting off the ground back to space, to the Moon! swinging test dummies around its far side. Our space ambition to launch humans, build a business, hauling payloads to the Moon to establish sustained presence on the lunar surface, a gas station fueling our future expeditions of the solar system. *That's our nature to explore*, get there first, learn to live. To survive. Then onward, to Mars and beyond. We don't know how easy it will be extracting water from moon rock. How much is actually there? We don't know. So many questions where we're going in the dark where we're returning our attention to the Moon.

IV

Milky Way Galaxy, 21st Century

While Earth kept turning, gravity held us close.
It was a very fine planet.

The night was too beautiful

to ever write a poem about—
stars out, satellites, cricket song—
the night too beautiful, memory a penstroke
of summer's air, the earth cooling silence.

What was it there that night too beautiful
for a common tongue, an owl-call, something
rustling in the bushes, a nearby mosquito
hum that night I sat in a lawn chair in
the dark, sky-watching for a comet's tail,
waiting for celestial sights. But then

a barn owl crossed overhead wing-wide
open, a different feral light too
                              beautiful—too
beautiful to ever write a poem about.

Remembered Lines on the Way to Stockton

My father owns the cattle on a thousand hills;
    they graze among windmills scattered
        along the interstate. Beneath a tinfoil moon

it's not quite dark by nine. A silver-sided truck
    roars, sucks at my passing car
        flashes high beams to let me over.

Bott's dots reflect the headlights,
    comets chased by tails along an asphalt skyway.
        I have traveled this road all the years of my life

a journey landscaped with exits never taken
    into countryside where mown hay swells blonde
        against alfalfa fields already regreening

and words rise from wild grasses
    like surprised birds or flock along power lines
        draped pole to pole beyond the city limit sign.

I pass the towers for a drawbridge.
    It no longer raises over its river
        the only ship a rowboat upended on the bank.

Faded letters on a grain tower
    advertise horses for sale. They died
        half a century ago.

There is no map for places such as these
    that recede in the rearview mirror
        and await my return. It is dusk

forever here, with the scent of mowing.
    Tonight I drive straight through to Stockton.
        My father's mansion has many rooms,

if it were not so I would have told you.
        A sudden farmyard hemmed
                by walnut trees. The rising thrum of cricket.

The Astronomer's Complaint

The night dreams itself, but no one wants to hear my visit to the house of the dead, not even morning's wide-eyed Moon growing bigger by the minute, sinking behind the bare oak, the blooming acacia moon-beamed yellow, a counter-glow. I have a headache. I can either see this page and not the Moon, or watch the Moon go down. Dissolving, an object of day, so pale I can glimpse it only because I know it should be there, faraway satellite so near. Always leaving. Always coming back, like dream and memory, like people I have loved. It hesitates, as if it might linger a bit more, listening. No building stands there, no person inhabits it, though it's just a matter of time. Even its dark side conquered, *Destination: Moon* a now-possible impossibility. It's like a jackpot, too many quarters pouring out. Everybody wants in. *My sweetheart's the man in the moon*, my mother would sing, washing dishes. I was too young. I believed her. I believed everyone felt that way. *I'm going to marry him soon* . . .

Zero Gravity

—space billionaires take flight

You leave Earth looking for perspective.
How you long to see it, the blue marble,

from outer space. The overview
changes everything astronauts say

and you are looking for change
to not take life so seriously. So much

energy required to get off the planet to
break with gravity, the bond with Earth

the ship violent with propulsion's inferno
shaking you loose from the known world.

But maybe your friend is right, maybe Earth's
best hope is mass conversions to religions

that teach reincarnation, then people might care
about the future of the planet? You unbuckle,

let yourself float free, wanting the thrill
before this once-in-a-lifetime trip ends,

even a few minutes of giddy weightlessness
so close to death, a tangible peril right

outside the window, Earth passing there
below you now, alone in the darkness.

What Childbirth and the Moon Landing Have in Common

Once the countdown begins, there is no turning back.

Such missions unfold in phases.

Both involve travel between worlds.

Both use the term "abort" if something goes wrong.

Someone's life is always at risk.

Follow the protocols.

Every stage must succeed for a good outcome.

Both birth and a lunar landing can be monitored at a distance by teams of experts via beeping screens.

Both involve extremely cramped quarters.

A uterus is somewhat like a lunar module, carrying its passenger through space protecting it from an inhospitable environment.

An astronaut enters zero-gravity; an infant will leave it behind forever.

At some point, each lets go of all they have ever known.

Heart rates go up.

Violent movements occur, like a ride on a giant roller coaster.

Under 10,000 pounds of thrust, the lunar module pitches and yaws, shaking like a tin can.

My mother said giving birth felt like someone pulling a suitcase out of her.

Neither the astronaut nor the fetus can survive the journey without an external life-support system.

Though astronauts have simulators to prepare them for what to expect, once the hatch opens, both humans enter realms they can't control.

At a certain point, all anyone else can do is watch.

A moon landing delivers a human body to the boundless dark of outer space; childbirth pushes a human body from darkness into blinding light.

Both arrive in alien worlds and require constant protection.

With childbirth, water cushions the departure. With the lunar spacecraft, water cushions the return to Earth.

Descending from the craft, the astronaut stands, tiny against the curvature of the enormous Moon; the infant, tiny astronaut, curls against the mother's breast.

You will never remember what it was like before either event occurred.

The face of the Moon, the face of the mother, forever changed.

The footprints never disappear.

Once upon a time I didn't go to Mars,

I didn't want to be an alien invader. On Mars I'd be the alien invading, though it turns out nothing lived up there back then. Plus it took nine weightless months in a cramped interplanetary ship not much bigger than a car. I'd never make it, stuck that long in outer space. And land on Mars? I had no desire to be in such a place. Everything red. Sky, dirt, rocks. Everything. Nothing. A frozen wasteland. I couldn't bear to look back at Earth—from Mars just a distant dot. Why leave home, colonize a world that's dead? We needed a backup planet, "life insurance for life as a whole," as a rich man said. But not everyone could flee a failing Earth. Who got on the starship with the practiced billionaires? Who had money for the one-way fare? The ticket buying multi-millionaires. Once upon a time

Space Travel Questionnaire: Know Before You Go

1. The universe, a vast expanse of empty space containing all of everything in existence, awaits. Would you say outer space is public or private?

2. Who owns the Earth, stars, the asteroids, the Moon, and all celestial bodies?

3. Is the international *Outer Space Treaty* of 1967 still in effect?

4. All countries who signed the treaty agree to avoid "the harmful contamination of space and celestial bodies." What would you consider harmful?

5. How do you define "terraformation?"

6. Which of the following did Apollo astronauts leave on the lunar surface: footprints; thermometers; a box of mirrors; lunar landers; an aluminum hammer; two golf balls; moon rovers; a falcon feather; family photos; 96 bags of poop; faded U.S. flags?

7. When we crash spent rockets into Mars, the Moon, or leave them adrift in space, is *that* contamination?

8. The treaty protects outer space and everything in it from national appropriation. Can a private company appropriate?

9. Who are the chief funders of space exploration?

11. How will mining firms extract, control, and sell resources from a celestial body they cannot own or contaminate according to the *Outer Space Treaty*?

12. The treaty establishes the use of space exclusively for peaceful purposes. What new branch of the Armed Forces did the U.S. form in 2019?

13. Why do scientists believe that civilizations always self-destruct?

14. Why is space called the final frontier?

Space Walk

Outside the spacecraft tethered by barely a thread, the astronaut swims in a sea of nothing far from any knowns, swaddled like an infant must be, flung out for science, for discovery, for repairs. A frontier, always what's next part of a grand adventure, home a frangible concept ever-rippling outward with her, unmoored in concentric circles. She's given herself to them, to the challenge, sometimes horror to see so much so clearly where she floats in low earth orbit traveling 28,000 kilometers per hour. An eerie stillness circling Earth every 90 minutes, enormous planet suspended in spacetime as she is suspended waiting to climb back aboard. Her life, hurtling through that vacuum, not flat as the world was once believed to be, even her DNA changing.

O celestial body, one of us, we peer beyond the edges of the cracked-ceiling world acquainted with the dark, speeding toward uncertainty, slipping the margins of time.

Moonlighting

The Moon at three-quarters needs help. She peers at me through the window. It's all in her expression. *You're a lunatic honey*, it implies, *but someone who might prove useful.* A moth batters across her trembly face. No one reaches to brush it away. *Oh*, her lips purse, *help me I'm falling, oh*, but I know better. Bland pie-face drained of color won't last. Sinking is what she's good at. Other nights she'll break onto the horizon, the broad who craves a spotlight, sequined smile, onstage for a curtain-call larger than life. I can't endure her final scene, how her eyebrows agonize. She bows out forehead first, the droop of her cheek drops *oh* and then *ah*—the art of resistance a flicker, a quicksilver tear, the tides swelling in silent applause. She can't get away fast enough.

"What they should have sent was a poet."

Frank Borman, Apollo 8, the first mission to orbit the Moon

. . . except Borman later said he hadn't said that, so maybe it was just what everyone else said he'd said. Or wished he'd said, wished so hard that someone decided he *had* said it? Because if you say something enough times . . . He definitely said, "the last thing I would have wanted on our crew was a poet," though this was years and years later. What he most remembers from halfway between the Moon and Earth was watching Earth rise out of the ink black of space, lifting over the Moon's bleak, dead landscape. A blue marble. A blue agate. "What they should have sent," Frank Borman did say, "was poets because I don't think we captured in its entirety the grandeur of what we had seen." The astronauts thought what they'd seen—Earth alone in empty space—would change everything. "It was small enough," he added, "you could cover it with your thumbnail."

He just didn't want a poet trying to fly the thing.

California, Transit

Every word will be an afterword.
That's a pretty little valley, I said to no one.

Maui Vacation in a Time of War

Which war? The pandemic had stalled. The man on the television said the end of the world had arrived so we packed suitcases. To Mars? No, ha-ha, to Maui. Take-off a miracle, such tremendous weight airborne. Then, the sun lifted above Haleakala, a parking lot rooster crowed, "it's bro-o-ken! it's bro-o-oken," and it was. We took pictures constantly. Would beauty remain? Beauty was doing fine without us. Beauty also knows something about destruction. Under the waves whales could be heard calling, moans too deep for words. The whales. We watched for them to blow and breech, which they did, their keiki too. We shouted *whales!* at every sight, clapping like children at a circus, the tail slaps, sometimes a dozen in a row.

But we wanted more—sea turtles, sacred animals. We hunted them down in a protected cove. They drew in their heads wanting nothing to do with our desire. Our iPhones. Our sunscreen. Yes, news got through, we could feel it in our feet. The surf washed the sand clean every night. Not a footprint remained. When we returned home, time had changed. We set our clocks an hour ahead, but it didn't help. The world was still ending, and it was beginning again at the same time.

Later, Lunch Near a Firing Range

On the porch, I eat a first drippy peach to the tune of birdsong. A breeze teases the windchime. Also on the plate, avocado toast. Somewhere else people go hungry, a hollow-eyed baby won't cry. A shooter activates. I take another bite. Let's say it. Here, it's an amazing afternoon. Except. Except for nearby explosions of gunfire. One is not more *is* than another. Overhead thin clouds form, not a drone in the sky. The yat-yat bird yat-yats while within earshot, people obliterate targets, like a war zone's gaping apartments, someone's body abandoned along the roadside. A good smell rises from the earth, and how thankful I am for the avocado on my toast . . . but not for the birdshit spotting the table. Against the windchime's pings, a gun fires steadily. Always both. A woodpecker taps. One full green dogwood leaf, heart-shaped, drifts to the ground for no reason. A bomb falls on a children's playground, on a train station. I don't want to go inside, but I'd like the shooting to stop. People wait in a line for water and bread. A neighbor, calling and calling, has lost her cat. Crows interrupt, "Here-here, Here-here!" "Now, Now, Now!" I haven't finished lunch. The gunfire continues. The sun ticks across the sky.

Quantum Time

Who even remembers July and
August went or where or how
it just did and too-soon Septembered
comes Fall Summer leaves left
leaves worry fall founders
the night rings no rain I ask
the trees for help go stand in the sun
wonder what a photon is it isn't
it is everything and nothing both
all of the time and sometimes one
Sun's energy spent wisteria pods
pop and shatter scattered seeds
hit the cement the difference between
what we see and what actually exists.

Sorrow Is Better Than Laughter

Ecclesiastes 7:3

She hadn't realized this herself. It was something she'd read and since it came from the Bible, she felt it must have some sense to it, but she wondered how this could be. Her sorrows, sometimes plentiful, seemed ordinary, what everyone endured from time to time—deaths, aging, loss, loneliness—but nothing like the really big tragedies these days with pandemic, wars, mass shootings, famine, floods. The news showed so much suffering, such sorrow, it was difficult to imagine, and the weight of it pressed down on her when she tried. She felt guilty, but that wasn't the same. Her own sorrows were supposed to be better than laughter and the verse went on to say it was because sadness of countenance made the heart glad. In the mirror she could see her countenance wore sadness more and more, the down-turned mouth, lines grown deeper. Because of this she guessed she was on her way to something better after all. She couldn't help noticing a lightness at the thought.

Lacunae

I am odd. I have a way with my pen but what of it.

My heart has a hole, everything five beats.

Toggling between hope and dread with fairly simple sentences.

Dimeter, trimeter, iambs, and trochees, the metrics mimic the blackbirds' call.

A pleasing pause and speed, how the meter trips lightly over a heavy line.

But what am I to do with this.

Looking for connections, the imagery doesn't connect. And then. And then.

Now it's a single line like a fortune or horoscope. A talisman, omen, something personally instructive.

An everyday magic in a very fast world, or is it just my superstitious mind.

Solitude, quietude, thermodynamics, chaos, floating, something new seems essential.

As if we hadn't lost several preposterous years, as if some will ever be enough.

To return briefly to the poem, where is the speaker, where the appropriate metaphor.

A voice you hear in the distance on calm nights.

The poem closes like a tunnel behind me.

There are 47 versions of the ending.

The poem is blades and knives.

It's about sound, silence, listening, and maybe the cooling of time. About waiting for the actual shoe to actually drop.

Penumbra: a marginal area. Isotropic: no innate direction. Entropy: disordered everything.

To return briefly to the poem, the last line imitates the first.

Those blackbirds flaw the sky.

Am I odd, finding my way with a pen?

After 108°, Two Owls, the Moon, a Wind in the Trees

Just after sundown, hot breeze rattles the hornbeams' tired leaves. Solo cricket starts, stops, and a large shadow drops close over my head, lands on the fountain. Another owl joins, two shadows now chuckling together soft in the dusk. One flies to a branch above me, first flicker of fear, imagined hooked claw and beak tightens until a swivel of its head. The other, a barely visible shape at its fountain perch, takes off over the back fence, breaking darkness with deeper darkness. The remaining owl follows, soundless. Quiet cricket resumes, quickens. I resume. All wind stopped now except breath, the trees, the nearly full moon shining through. Praising not the heat, not the dark. Not the silence. I praise the interventions.

Once upon a timepiece

we were four and five,
    marvelous beings
who could do anything,
    not whimsy but certainty
be anything, something
    utterly boundless, a bird
a dinosaur, a doctor,
    a UFO. We were
four or five once upon a
    timetable, our bodies
marvelous beings worn
    with easiness changed
from flesh to fur to fin to
    flight, the sky thick
enough to walk across
    from any window,
the window of our eyes.
    Once, the timing
of days of nights running
    counter to any clock
in great fields waiting,
    sheets of darkness
robes of merciful light
    spun of deep grassiness
tunnels and waves, whatever
    we lifted in our hands.
Once upon a tincture,
    once upon a tinderbox
we romped upon marvelous,
    being certain nothing
would change for us
    unless we wanted it to.

for my brother

Quantum Theory

Lost against a backdrop of stars, lost all daily notion of now, zero gravity, time's experience warped by my spectator approach, do you feel it, the continuum, how relativity accepted must link to quantum theory, the theory behind the smallest actions in the universe impossible to comprehend but possible to imagine through thought experiments otherwise known as poems. Otherwise not languageable though scientists say it explains practically everything. I hope it speaks to someone. And if there are no further questions, will it suffice to find words that make the world look like what it feels like? I can't tell over Zoom, one man listening from a garage, others don't turn on their videos. Someone else arrives too late to care. But I have a wristwatch now. It follows the Moon.

It's About Time

Exactly one hundred years after photos of a solar eclipse proved Einstein's theory of general relativity back in 1919, (*stars askew in the heavens!*)—a theory which also predicted the existence of black holes—scientists release the first image captured of one: a burning eye peers back from deep space.

The smell of space is a burnt-out vacuum, an astronaut once said.

Besides black holes, relativity implies the possibility of time travel, time looping back on itself. Sleep, too, suspends time, delivers us unknowing to the future while memory takes us instantly into the past, and what we know is what we don't know.

"Science is a wonderful thing if you don't have to earn your living at it," Einstein said. The same can be said for writing.

A mathematical equation chalked on a blackboard is an elegant way to express thought without words. So, too, a musical score carries a symphony without making a sound, while numbers on a clock merely trace the local perception of unquantifiable time.

Einstein's divine distraction, the violin, allowed him to suspend time and thought through music, entering the flow, its embedded mathematics joined with the body's movement, a musical measure of time.

A physicist once told me it would take 40,000 years to establish a precise convention for the meaning of "now."

Einstein knew his theory also predicted the existence of gravitational waves. Scientists announced their detection in 2016, cosmic disturbances created by the collision of two black holes, the fabric of spacetime shaken like a quilt.

Gravitational waves create detectable sound, the acoustics
of spacetime, the past ringing right past us.

You think you want to stop time, but some story is always just
beginning.

Time is distorted by matter, by the presence of heavy objects. Time
stretches and contracts. What does this mean?

We are star stuff pondering the stars, according to Carl Sagan. And
so within our elemental core, we know our furthest ancestors are
the fiery stars and why it is we seek heaven among them.

Maybe all Einstein ever really wanted was to know what time it
was.

Enumerating the Sublime

after "Thirty-six Views of the Moon," by Ala Ebtekar

thirty-six discrete frames arranged on a wall

        a circle—white—afloat in cyan blue emerges

    the full Moon full of its astonishments

its face broken by rectangle views, by empty space

            the human gaze refracted

   Earth's familiar satellite

            Moon mirroring illusions

we see the there that's not

O

Drink wine and look at the moon
and think of all the civilizations the moon has seen
passing by,

      the poet wrote a thousand years ago

how many more have passed by since then

       now people build cities on the Moon

  we will drink wine and look up

     we will see civilizations passing over our heads

  how many glasses of wine

     how many more will pass

  the Moon in pieces looking back

Efforts at a New Season

Clouds track across fresh sky, the first muddied footprints of spring.

I speak of fish and desire and abrupt release.

I remember the unremembered dream.

What rises up from the earth, the land skinned of meaning?

I have lived four lives already. It's just that everything can't work at once.

Time moves, an imperceptible legato, the speed that ink dries.

Something too remarkable to throw away.

I've known since I was a child, we can't discover the language of the skies.

That which is hidden beneath the ordinary surface of life, marked by changes. The comfort that is found in solitude.

Begin dreaming a new vernacular.

Round a curve and the land unclenches an open palm before you.

Sound is married to time: neither remains.

Clouds mumble among themselves and whisper in the mountain's ear. Their shadows creep.

Just like that a cloud blocks the sun completely.

We have always lived in dark times. You don't have to be special to survive.

Coming Close,

after Charles Wright

light seen beneath the waves
glints against suspended sand.
A giant sea turtle appears
swims past so near
in the sun-streaked waters—

Honu, sacred creature,
I can't translate wonder.
I can't say anything new.
Why do I wrestle with words
long after you've gone?

And the little waves say *sh-sh-h-h* to me,
and the big waves say, *go home.*
The sand says . . . nothing. And the Moon
trailing after the morning says
see, see? without making a sound.

Quantum Leap

Startled bluebird swoop
from feeder to post what
wingbeats blueredblur how
describe that instant
between here and not
the jump itself minor
in time and space a shock
in existence not presence
nor absence an interlude
of being probable like between
systole and diastole call it
beating one nanosecond
begun at some point will
stop hand on my breast
not mechanical but a synapse
like thought the not
known before I write
the next word the bird feeder
waits at the heart of the
Universe possibility hovers

Spacetime

We'll move from present to past in the near future, my husband says.
The past is always looking for us, says my aunt, 99 years old.
The past never is, I reply.

Coda

In spring, I'm afraid. Everywhere life rises again, noisy, brisk, airy green. There is no stopping it, at least not yet. I want to be that reckless, to throw my self noisy into the warming days. So much lost, I can't help wearing winter like a necklace—to know where the season leads, the end of growth, the waning of life. It may not seem like courage to let go of confinement, the safe and quiet room, the dark seed, the eggshell. To pick up again and head out an open door. It is to reawaken, to leave behind the dream life, trade it for, yes, life to live, to lose.

There are only two or three human stories, and they go on repeating themselves as fiercely as if they never happened before.

—Willa Cather

Notes

"California, April" and additional haiku-ish section openers are after Robert Hass' poem, "Iowa, January."

"For Valentine's Day": The phrase "dreamy divagation" is from Elizabeth Bishop's poem, "Moose."

"To Calculate the Color of the Sky": The epigraph is from the article, "You Think You Know What Blue Is, But You Have No Idea," by Lucy Huang, *Inverse.com*. The terms *Excelsior* and *E pluribus unum* were invoked frequently as part of then-New York Governor Mario Cuomo's daily televised encouragement offered to the country at the height of the pandemic in the absence of any such guidance offered by the then-U.S. President.

"This Is What It Looked Like When We Got There": The remarkable June 2020 video of a string quartet performing to plants in the Barcelona Opera House can be viewed on YouTube. https://www.youtube.com/watch?v=i9BRbtIgipQ

"Quarantine": Based on an article by Julia Prodis Sulek, "For coronavirus-stricken cruise passengers, dread over second quarantine ahead," *The Mercury News*, March 9, 2020.

"Litany in a Time of Contagion": After Thomas Nashe's poem, "A Litany in Time of Plague."

"July, How Far I Fly": The title is from the song "Cuckoo!" by Benjamin Britten.

"A Question While Watching Birds" is composed as variations on the haibun. The Czeslaw Milosz quote is from his poem, "Meaning."

"Last Flight Out": Helicopter pilot Dan Alpiner's photo inspired this poem and can be viewed online at https://www.wildlandfirefighter.com/2020/10/16/owl-lands-inside-helicopter-battling-californias-creek-fire/

"Quantum Sense" is dedicated to the memory of Joseph P. Ashton and considers migratory birds' use of quantum effects in their eyes to navigate their global journeys.

"Listening to Mars": Listen here: https://www.youtube.com/watch?v=yT50Q_Zbf3s. Thanks to Susannah Ashton for sending the video my way.

"4.6 Billion Years" first appeared in print in *The Polaris Trilogy* anthology as part of the Lunar Codex. As such, it's scheduled for launch to the Nobile Crater, Lunar South Pole, Nov. 2024.

"The Unreached Paradise of our Despair": Title is taken from Byron's *Childe Harold,* st. CXXII, and is dedicated to the memory of Dr. Harvey Birenbaum.

"We Are Going" is NASA's Artemis Mission hashtag.

"What Childbirth and the Moon Landing Have in Common" is inspired by Dr. James Joki, a former NASA flight controller who worked on wearable life support systems for the Apollo 11 moonwalk and eventually became an obstetrician. *Seattle Times,* June 16, 2019.

"What they should have sent was a poet": Quotes from Frank Borman are from the film "Earthrise" and from an interview with David Kestenbaum of *This American Life.*

"Enumerating the Sublime" is written in response to Ala Ebtekar's moonscape collage, "Thirty-six Views of the Moon." The poem cited is by Omar Khayyam, 11th century mathematician, astronomer, and poet.

"Coming Close" is after Charles Wright's poem, "Clear Night."

"Spacetime" is dedicated to my time-traveling aunt and namesake, Lorelle Light, born 1924.

Acknowledgments

Thank you to the following publications in which poems from *Listening to Mars* first appeared, sometimes in a slightly different form:

Axon Journal: "For Valentine's Day," "The Unreached Paradise of Our Despair," "Quantum Migration"

Breathe: 101 Contemporary Odes, C & R Press. "Remembered Lines on the Way to Stockton"

Caesura: "Efforts at a New Season"

Dancing About Architecture and Other Ekphrastic Manoeuvres (Cheshire, MA: MadHat Press, 2024): "Enumerating the Sublime"

Dreaming Awake: New Contemporary Prose Poetry from the United States, Australia, and England, ed. Peter Johnson and Cassandra Atherton (MadHat Press, 2023): "This Is What It Looked Like When We Got There," "Quarantine," "A Jigger of June," "Sky Writing"

EcoTheo Review: "Coda," "Zero Gravity"

Inflectionist Review: "The Still Center of the Galaxy," "Surviving Solstice"

Jung Journal: Culture and Psyche: "Last Flight Out" (first appeared as "That guy should buy a lottery ticket").

Moon City Review: "July, How Far I Fly"

Polaris Trilogy Anthology and Lunar Codex Project: "4.6 Billion Years." Launching Nov 2024 to Nobile Crater, Lunar South Pole via SpaceX Falcon Heavy / Astrobotic Griffin Lander / NASA VIPER Rover

Poetry Flash: "Quantum Theory," "Space Walk," "Quantum Leap"

Rattle: Poets Respond: "Listening to Mars"

Red Wheelbarrow: "Fiction, 101"

Reed Magazine: "This Was Also True"

Salt: "It's About Time"

the museum of americana: "What Childbirth and the Moon Landing Have in Common," "What they should have sent was a poet"

Poets seem to write the most inclusive, often effusive acknowledgements to their new books, listing anyone who touched the work as it made its way from inspiration to print. Partly because poetry is a communal artform from its roots in oral tradition, partly because a poetry collection is an incremental genre written syllable by syllable, poem by poem, with a variety of interlocutors shaping and encouraging the work along the way, a process often covering years. But it's also because the process of finding a publisher requires such perseverance that anyone who kept our hopes afloat deserves undying gratitude. We made it. Thank you Universe!

Therefore, a huge shout-out to publisher Dr. Ross Tangedal and Cornerstone Press, who believed in this work and made it a beautiful book, and to each of the student editors involved. And thank *you* reader for your time and attention, for buying and reading *Listening to Mars*. It's not an exaggeration to say the book wouldn't be here if it weren't for Kelly Sicat and precious studio space at Montalvo Arts Center offering time away from the pandemic, time to see what I had. Thank you to Frank, Erika Howsare, and Annie Kim, my first readers, to Betsy Johnson and Mary Donnelly, and to Nils Peterson who said, "Send it." My appreciation to all the editors whose individual acceptances listed above helped me believe in the project, but especially Cassandra Atherton, Peter Johnson, and Anne Cheilek. Thanks Holly Iglesias and those already mentioned for your generous blurbs.

Most of these poems were written during the pandemic years. Thank you to Alan Soldofsky who invited me to sit in on a couple of his Zoom courses, extending that vital community; to Revathi Krishnaswamy for timely support; and thanks to my own Zoom students sharing Joy during those difficult days.

How do we make sense of any dark time? Through family, friends, and our larger communities who keep showing up. My glints of light.

Thank you all.

SALLY ASHTON is a writer, teacher, and editor-in-chief of *DMQ Review*. Author of four previous books, including *The Behaviour of Clocks* (2019), Ashton specializes in brief forms across genres. Her work has appeared in numerous journals and anthologies and is headed to the Moon in 2024. She served as Santa Clara County Poet Laureate (2011-2013).